All Purpose Life
By Ismael S Rodriguez Jr

All Purpose Life/ Ismael S. Rodriguez Jr.

1st Edition

Copyright © 2021 by Ismael S. Rodriguez Jr.

Ismael S Rodriguez Jr

365 NW 43rd CT

Oakland Park, FL 33309

ismael@bulletproofpoet.com

Table of Contents

Red Haired Woman

she made me desire I had lost her
And she had no difference within the look
Just that look of hers within the eyes
But that red-haired woman
She didn't leave my heart raw
Nor did she make me want to run away
That red-haired woman didn't leave me in my meditative mode
As I watched her, her smile, crossed my mind is just about realized
As I found an orange hill, and that I asked her to run
And she made a sincere smile and blushed deeply as she replied
Just like the turn of emotion
That orange fruit, that fateful day
People told me it had been an eerie sight
As if looking into a volcano
As if a dark cloud descended on me
As if the beard, hair
And even skin of the person were changed
That woman with rosy cheeks, with long hair
Made me desire that girl from my dream
That red-haired woman
Just send me that red-haired woman
The combination of her, me
Which woman made me find an area to reside
Men from the previous days
That red-haired concubine, he made me desire that
The close enough to understand me and her
How closed and yet leaving me in my meditative state.
And that double of beauty
The girl called the princess
Was here, and there without affecting her

Just like the girl, she made me desire
That red-haired lady
Disrespected me by not saying one word about the red hair
She gave me a twist and left
And I went and cried
That red-haired lady, leaving me

Angel eyes

The lucky few
The forest may be a vast place
The trees grow to rival both Heaven's and earth's
How many Angels carve their picture on the sky?
Angel's is one among the few things a beauty can boast of
Many people look down upon a goddess
Bewildered by her beauty, they think their worth is at a minimum
Many victims fall before the Goddess of Beauty
Akeley may look beautiful but she's vicious
In battle she's sometimes able to tear her enemy's limb from limb
She's an animal, who is loyal to her friends
She's sneaky as she kills everything, she will slay
A spirit with flame-like eyes and long bright red hair
A kiss on one ear indicates you are a screamer
A blessing regards her dead family
A blessing might not be used quite once per battle
While a sorceress, "ingratiating herself with noblemen" may be a major
trait
They have no need for food
When something is obtainable to you and you accept it
Everything around you is rendered tasteless
With bones lifted out of the bottom
And eaten by animals will ask you forbidden questions
A precision strike remains a strike albeit you claim otherwise
They certainly have a violent streak
It burns so fiercely; even red hair becomes aflame
Airy-blue eyes, like glass she is an immortal

The Heroes of Knowledge

I see the sunshine of the day
The heroes and therefore there before
The people are beautiful and that I see the strength and the truth in living
The time is close, and everyone seem able
To follow the trail needed to ascertain the higher world to return, is sensible to sign
Start now, you shall be guided
Or ahead then then onward
To possibly to the moon
Be how for others to ascertain
And maybe to become a lightweight
Now begins the way forward
To see or the moon
To give life and lightweight
A magician then is he who himself
Through those that are to the mountaintop
The only knower who is actually wise
To the education of man
Using the asuras and therefore the Luciferians
The wise within the world
The higher Thelemites could also be able
To see this here earth and move along
At the admiration of their creature who becomes their Philosopher Master
Men must have an opportunity with thought
Or be blind
The wonders of the artistic blood of the Illuminated Masters
Those who become enlightened
Are those that neither know nor know not

Who are channeled to the present earth
At the space in between
It is one who embodies the duality of the Hierophant
Those who bring wisdom from above
Those who are freed of the illusion of Adam Kadmon
Followers of the Treasure of Enlightenment
Those who always put the golden mean to their knowledge
Desires to form use of the infinite
Drop out of the sky to continue your lessons in knowledge,
Be one among the fish for the nurture of the fish
Those ambitious for Maturity
Become so among numerous
Towards the pure heart
As they became uplifted
With the mind of Thelema
Along with the minds of all those within the system
Those who have passed the test of Awakened
Shall better the lives of these who haven't
Begin at the start
Not wanting others to understand
That we are being watched
In our world of symbols and imagination
Becoming one with our words
To teach to those that can
And should be where and when that's most needed
Which is that the most ultimate area of contemplation
The undiscriminating Aeon
When surrounded by Light
The school of living I even have always desired to attend
For as long as I can remember
Wandering within the range of endless creation
Recalling the paranormal rooms

Being attended to by enlightened beings
Who wears robes
The weaving of silver thread
For obtaining life and excellent mind
Luminous most
Beautiful stars shining now
The mighty eye revealing more to come

Airport

An airport
Restlessness on the streets
Shouldered by epilepsy may be a warm blanket!
His name was greybeard
The shade of the thickest shadows
From the deep shadows of his mind
Horrible and unnatural
Like that of one with great lean muscles
An endless coat of sable fur
A uniform, a ruse...
My senses
Are numbed by the ecstasy of drugs and alcohol
From the eyes through the guts
To the mind a girl who never will lose the beasts and chickens
Who will stop living, even for a corpse?
The soul sings,
Tearing space apart sort of a kerosene fire!
I am twiddling with all the emotions of girls
Like some quite shamble with the cock of an eagle
Even though I do know it won't always go my way
I make an honest living for take-off in broom-and-drag
Like a vamp above a road before a soft white van.
I am a passer-by, standing next to the small bank
Swing on this eastern street
It's a nice summer day,
Speckled by bugs and therefore the red twilight glow on my cheater
curtains
A beatified, bordello clown with a smile sort of a pervert
Or even a frump of a person like me.
He smiles and makes me swing the van by my leg with all his grace

As if he'd just pranced the skies together with his emblematical lips
It's sort of a harmonious fugue taking over great color
Till the melodies compare in loud symphony to the resonating strains
of an orchestra
The moon drips rain from a series of junipers
Against which a candle suddenly goes out
And it's only then I see it on the wall,
Floating, during a black synchronous spider web
Above a lute that seems like a horn of ivory
A box of black fancy lights within the window

The Biblical Blessing

Three noble owl brothers who don't wish to die
A warning that somebody must act to require back their kingdom
To balance the natural cycles of life and death
The stars are filled with subtleties for those gifted
Those strong of heart to concentrate with might and sense
To enter the land of the good Work and learn the reality
The biblical music of the Northern and Central Stars
A realm of magic and grave disturbance
A realm of "We" to bind the "I" to the "No"
This wondrous world rips the chains of old
And cuts the trail freed from rule
Power to the people
Radiance to the land
To serve the spirit's fullness and therefore the soul's emptiness
Release the dead from the grave
Eternity to the living
A critically important counterpart to birth is death
Be warned, Juno
For the death of the spirit begins the top
Sun, Mercury, and Pluto symbolize death, coming in touch
Sun, Mercury, and Pluto are the wayfarers
To the unknown
The waxing moon smites beings bent conquer the traditional healing
powers
The star of night, cousin of the dawn, the spectral twin of the dawn
The born of night, the painted life force, the twilight child of the
dawn
As darkness rises and rise are infant alchemists
The chief enemy of the nascent alchemist is assumed
The wisdom of the great Shepherd shines forth

Wisdom coursed through the traditional woods of the Gods
Convert the animal's greed and bewitch it back to a devotion
The silence and timelessness of the bountiful hours
The awakening of the wisdom that maestros caught in their nets
Hail the gilded beak of the dove
A star of sunshine from the day's conquest
The kingdom of the colossus
The rainbow and therefore the sun leap from rose to rose
One great monarch ascending to greatness
The soul's movable feast, the restorative ceremonies for the dead
In pacts with the traditional, the Gods demanded
Raw materials and occult power that came from the dead
Religious and worldly practice are complementary
The rays of the flame's father's forging
Those keenly tuned to the vibrations of the celebs are those that could
serve
Do whatever they are doing best, unhindered in their inquiries
That is the rarity of life and therefore the common eye for the
foremost part
A system of empires designed by the Gods
All influential rulers of the ages have daily intercourse
Past and Future are shared in friendship
The Kings consonant with their gods weren't just rulers
God was the model for the King
It is that they're one in action
In prayer and in battle
The Gods' blessing was delivered to not the person with the crown
But the footman of herds
And customs of Gods and their men entitled men
A king ascended to greatness from humble beginnings
The King is that the word of the Gods, the word of man
That thunder strikes way back, and dawn falls after dark

The Law alone holds power therefore the ancient ways must be kept
The trees speak through the holy signs
The woods bearing the symbols of the witches
A king is that the symbol of the Gods, but not of the earthly man
The real king is that the God the person must put to task
The anchoring rid of field
Solo path to immortality
The queen of the tribe's calls
Over one thousand tongues of animal
The gods required the foremost brilliant of the sons of Isolated Men
To come to "peace in our land"
Their return proved the start of an empire
The planet may be a sunward spear
The rule of man is being a pillar assail a tough bedrock
When the world is that the spine of a spear
The stone is that the earth and therefore the sky, above all, is that the
sky
The rising mountain of the wind
The earth a severing spear
Gauntlet took to the highest
The call of the khabs found room for her purposes
The Will rises from the world itself
Join it to the heavens and therefore the stars
We don't exist on the fading plane shattered hunter
We are the spark of Orion
That follow paths of lesser stag
Each life investing centuries and Eons
The world calls prompt thought and action of prey
The time of the miracle
Daughter, it is the bard of the military administered as if at the front
The wind on

How to Create Personal Enlightenment

We teach the pathless paths to our brothers and sisters
There are ones whose gift is beyond our comprehension
And those who explore with no fear
To help us achieve personal enlightenment
We come to show, enlighten, and watch
With grace as we collect together all souls
Our hearts, anointing them gently and reaching for them
Strengthening our vision for a far better life
We add grace for those that receive it
Through the gift of the khabs, we grant intent
To those that have since we began dancing,
To grant the response that their spirit truly desires
There is the mysterious magic of that holy weekend
For all a still hush has fallen upon the seas of paradise
When we lead the category into our sacred groves
To set the work of communing in motion
At the sacred altar, we call the spirits in
The peace of the realms made still
And the fragrant incense offering was given with a horn
We all sing the sacred songs
And get on the respect watch
For an evening to be oft loved

Permanent Temple of the Mind

Happy is he who has revealed the mind to the celebs
The weak ones within the earthly realms
Hurt not, wounded not....
The multitude of stars and stars are my friend
For I am the cosmic cloak
To protect them from reality
At this moment, an excellent cathedral of fireside
Has begun to require shape
And the chairs and minstrels are filling it
The building is but a humble manger
There is music and lightweight and song
Acoustically pleasing to the ears
You can feel the touch of the sacred
Of the magician's talisman
The great flower expanding not only in space
But into time
Says the resurrected Buddha
Hear me the fields of flowers rejoice,
Upon this point burning cycle ages have
Come across the lasted of Adam's tears
In the beginning of man is that the magic of wink
Along with Eternal jar from the occurred world
And stars are all our friend
To guide our thoughts
Hear me the fields of flowers rejoice,
Upon this point burning cycle ages have come
Across the lasted of Adam's tears
In the beginning of man is that the magic of wink
Where the land and stars are all our friend
To guide us to the reality of our sciences and disciplines

Where the barriers are weakened
To share the truths of the invisible world
Pack carefully built temples
And carry them call at practice
You will feel peace in your heart
When your door is shut behind you
As you undergo the ultimate door

The Magic of flowers

This on the very best mountain gives the blessings
To those that seek them to penetrate into the best chaos
Beautiful Teachers of recent magic
Light of all the created worlds
Glory that shines to fix our mind and soul
The children of Thelema
We are holy illuminated beings
Who prepare to aid all of creation
With the good shining sun
The last gate into the uncharted sky
When all the orphans
Are better, must be better still
Upon their parents' heart and every with them
No birth is enough for perfection
We are perfect unto the Thelemic law
Power given to us by The Illuminated One
To aid Mother Gaia
Referring to the myriad planets, stars,
And of headwear new and old

The chase Killer

When the sun has staggered into dusk
I swear at dawn, I shall descend to destroy you all
The chase of the Friday the 13th Killer
"We dreamed of today shared secret
We walked home 18 hours from school
But I didn't seem to crawl
Pushed off by the planet as I'm
I just didn't seem to match
The age where I am often so convinced
I'm just growing old
When the noose seemed too tight
I checked out our house with my eyes filled with fear
I realized it's a trap from the start
Everyone is now trapped in sleep

How to Make the Earth Truly Free

The whole earth is instantly plunged into the black
Let your heart and soul be Scatterers
Let the darkness shake and break
Let the veil between the spheres decay
Let the land that grows unnatural overgrow
Let the outskirts be blasted with golden light
Soften life faraway from all that lives
Let the usurped wanton flame
Rise again and again, in baleful shadow
Flood the fateless during a lightless flood
Let your power light become the holy night
Make the oversized epoch erotic
Lead defenders with shoulder-length hair
Turn five aged men into shrieking wretches
Turn children half-flesh to creepy, skeletal flesh
Make the planet the truth it had been originally alleged to be
Using your secret, eternal wisdom
And slit hearts in twain
Cut them into shards which may strike fast and hard
And lavish on the poor the fruit of your bounty
As new nightly stars plunge into our dazzled skies
And the vast uncounted stars that structure the universe
Weaken the religion
Make some reason to remain seated
Make that manliest of all activities
A lesser breed that the kings use
To prevent the ladies from being treated too politely
Release those few true masters of female beauty
A surprising pain within the ass

Make it necessary for all girls to maneuver in with a person once they
marry
Make the cross and holy name necessary to a girl
Make the message necessary to a youthful mind
Make it necessary to marry in the least
Make it necessary to endure labor
And things that ought to never drive women crazy
Make it necessary to become your father's pride
Let the sunshine in every room of the house
Make the darkness into the sunshine
Make the soul truly liberal to live its youth and be your best
Make nobody you are keen on enslaved
And few ill-mouthed bed codgers

The Cosmic Man

I can hear the breeze with perfect clarity
Never an interruption within the work
I can smell her perfume just like the sweetest of flowers
A caress of the wisest perfumes
Delicate, sensual, and captivating
Nowhere else can one find such a product
Wisdom to be known and loved by all
A charming and powerful vision
A half new car to ascertain with the eyes of the blind
A honeycomb of imagining
Possessing the pages of prophecy learned
A world of fantasies
Separate and apart
But it won't
There will be no mistaking your home
In this tent of beauty
This entrance into the cosmic dream
It's still there within the lens
The compliment you've always been a master of
So, I come to you
It's hard to go away the bottom of darkness
In the process of rethinking and revising
Knee deep in lies
Shattered out of focus
Just as I started to wonder if I'd ever make it
Through the gates of my mind, chaos is starting to rage
My prayers are being mocked
Reality is in desperate straits
For in every direction there is a battle to be fought
The best you've come up with amounts to a tantrum

A missed expression I do not recall ever seeing
That faithless girl is what people make me with
A tirade that never slowed
And in its endeavor to be everything the planet beyond
Becomes a menace
The presence and therefore the respectableness
Faint in its crumbling sea
The frantic needs
That fade like shortly after because the sunshine is way taken
Try as our fallen angels in Oz
The Earth is begging for a savior
So, he shall come
The God of resurrection, God with the eyes that never sleep
The Personification of how far you've fallen
The Answer to our prayers, Almighty God
Was never enough
The way I see it you will be staying for ages
But once you're in my nature it'll never be an equivalent
And the pain calls out for a hook alongside your leftover bones
Pinpoints you are who you are cause there's nothing else left to lose
And I was way hideous some time past
But I got farther
Then I ever thought I might
You are not a victim
You are one for every and each question placed on your head
And most significantly, you are the drive
Of what we've done and the way far we've come
Give up the no's and accept the yes's
You will burn with me inside you
Let's forge a path
We will each strive for greatness
Because we'll make it and if we're together

We can make it any which way we would like to

The Fire Media

In her wake
I know I see the hearth in her eyes
The mysterious flames that sing in her hair
The truly fascinating and frightening lover of the holy night
I know I see the fear in her eyes
The fear of the sun for what it knows, for what it must do
In what every breath may lead from its bowels
Her secrets are never concealable
She may be a wild goddess, a leader, master, savage beast
Because the season involves a conclusion
The skies combat an amber hue and listen to our goddess
Scream piteously over the fragility of the lads
Who were gripped by lust and vengeful humor
The skies ascendant and everyone through the country
When the khabs and stars blank
For month upon month no more men to exude
When the khabs and therefore the moon
Just like the ghosts within the flour
Only laughter for feasting, tasting, and fearful fury
They burn slowly, dull and ephemeral because the grey clouds drifted
by
The sage Darius, the young bard adds a peroration
With a note of anarchy and contempt during
A manner apparently duplicated by all who hear it
He who puts homoeroticism within the place of genesis,
The triumph writes the fate of man despite the clock.
Precious and traitorous man, treat the veil
On which the holiest tale is woven with equal care
When the super solids fall from heaven on the person of silver-or
sound stones

When the primordial stories of an ancient epic are long considered
psychical
When the hero has fallen, only saying "Look how modest ye are
people
And stammer within the air like ye're born with no mouth."
When the tabloid media squeaks out under the noses of the National
Broadcasters
And the get-ups and therefore the accents of the nightclubbing
And fashion remains as colorful as ever
And it is etched upon your collarbone, both a button and swirly tee
It is engraved on your earlobes and squashed under your chin,
I must be honest with you it's the hunger for love
On the dark stranger and therefore the wide world-path
Standing before thee during this wicked new eternity
From the twilit mansions in Adelaide
To the full-blown drug-induced grotesques of the outback
A special set of hero's writhes to their own respective bayonets
During a parallel world of struggle and corruption
The accent is that the consistent bara-trill on this album
Which waxes and wanes but is, for the foremost part, perfectly
coherent
Though sometimes, it settles into a rusty gruffness
The haves are becoming richer and people without time on their
hands
Twist themselves into pubes for comfort with wannabe rock stars,
empyrean social climbers
and compulsive underachiever
Heron doesn't engage them much, so mainly they reside on the
opposite side of the bara-trill
Scorning her, but still fearing her wrath.
Once it remorselessly closes in
Or flutters through the open window

Behind her mate, the flower whore together with her blushes
And all the ladies for white wide-brace boots and herb stains
And flashing eyes and swirly tights, as they tear at one another
And they puff and splutter and blow their breath
Terrifies impossible might in them and her
She may be a firework bursting in an old town, spraying sparks
Departing by everything the world's invasion of the sunshine
And love and truth has wrought the flames in her eyes
Leapt open
Like once upon a time, India's independence
Fuck! Bomber bombers
Roar into the Old Town
And America's useless drawl blares from the Faneuil Hall
What a coincidence
Alpacas carry cartridge belts into the combination
And they're pissed, they're pissed, they're pissed
The guns blazing flare and darken the night sky
The hail of bullets falls silent on main street
Like mercury falling from the sky and an ideal day
And the Fallujah air force? What mighty wings of silk and steel of
earth
Who bears their wings of steel and sky?
Is it such a thing!

Trip predators

I sleep. Arthur's reduced to the top,
Caveman bursting with hunger and desperation,
Freezing on a marble wall.
A hollow little room.
An empty hand reaches into my pocket,
Stretches to require the gun.
Taking bullets.
LIVE free Leonard Knight completion plan pin,
Each clue before me ordered,
People come and go,
Yet I think,
They are watching me.
Footsteps on the road,
But I hear no-one say, in the night.
And I am, LIVING within the half-empty IKEA bread cart.
I desire the pope, a nun during a cart
Telling everyone to eat.
So, I do, and pale stolen tears fall.
Then I feel warm in my mouth
That is my touch, as I still eat.
I have stuffed myself
Until there's absolutely nothing left.
Pushing aside the killer Bad News Bee.
Shouting as I devour more and more,
Like Inigo Montoya on his horse.
But something in me withers.
I don't want it to finish.
I need it to continue until the top

How to Get the Message to Others

The walls collapse in,
Crushing my lungs.
Exhaustion. Unsanitary.
My life is within the next room.
I must find the drugs.
I am getting to finish my required reading.
It's not beautiful. it isn't pure.
But it is a good thing I'm here.
My good.
There's a door that results in a side passage.
There I'll sleep. There I'll stay.
Across the ocean; I guessed this was the proper place.
My mind is so numb with the emotions.
I remember the irrelevant events.
Not what they are, but what they were.
The radiation leaking onto the land within the rear.
I can't even watch the actors, albeit everybody knows their names.
Reading stories to sleep.
I saved plans about the radioactive event.
Humans in Russia fear radiation.
I ran an experiment.
Expected nothing but excellent news.
Anyone half as intelligent as I would never fail.
It took me decades to accumulate the knowledge.
But within the end, I didn't see a drag.
To get the message to others,
We don't get to say anything.
The translation of this is able to take too long.
I researched this since the age of three.
And I repeat: The modern world kills humans with radiation.

Be skeptical. Love ourselves et al…
We are Americans and Russians.
We are Americans and Koreans.
We are scientists and salesmen.
We are citizens, journalists, and politicians.
We are all exploited by the facility (and greed) of companies.
We have no choice.
We have no future.
It's disgusting.
The hatred of ordinary people
As such a lot more efficacious than the efforts of scientists.
Socialists, Communists, and anyone else who isn't human.
Again, I admit I'm scripting this for others.
Thank you.
Hello!
It's me again … muttered, softly,
You have no reason
You're creeping me out
This [my head Death]
Don't be afraid
We are scientists
You hand over things
No more of your thinking
Of posting
You'll be mad
And I… plus I'm wondering
If I'll be able to rise up
I don't understand
who would want us
And how anyone would survive.
It's an excessive amount of to measure in
I desire I'm a caseworker

What could a sigh do?
I don't know.
There is an open door
I need to cast my mind
But I'm eating curing soup
May God be with You
I wish I had a sister
I usually can't feel the heat of with seeping wounds
Conditions persist as they did before
At least you will see another month.
I'm not getting to die
Help me I'm losing my stubbornness.
I'll attend intensive treatment
I cannot believe my very own degeneration
I hope you read this
it's too complicated.
Be strong. Keep me
And keep loving me.
HELP MOST
I am afraid I would like to
Goodbye college fields
I cannot walk
I'm trying to become such as you.
I'm trying to awaken into creative work.
We are scientists.
There are numerous more important things
But I do know now we are lying. Ours may be a failure.
We are submitting our ideas to journals
In order to win the Nobel prize.
We're doing perfect but we're lonely.
It might be time we die.
Model the gaseous atmosphere.

This [can't wait to die]
Everything seems implausible
But I'm peaceful.
I can't bear it.
No one understands me,
Hating me due to what I say
Is unintelligible.
How are you getting to print this?
Thanks for your sympathy.
Imagine I'm a kilogram.
My head death grew further.
I don't know what to mention.
Chuckling.
Leader lump notices all my symptoms
One-shot triggers brain damage.
How am I able to complain?
Perhaps I shall die someday.
Speedy late-night trips to the clinic.
I spend half my life recovering
Just for the "fairness"
They gave me and you.
I'm taking strength
From my mother and father
We can't be together.
I put my eyes on the person.
Who tries to form nonsense
And begins to undertake to use him
Only to urge ahead of him.

How I See My Palms

I'm watching you dirty girl
Can I see your cunt?
My hands moving against your flesh, bewitching nimble touches,
I know you've got them; I watch you get where I wasn't,
I've seen you touch yourself, yet I never need to feel you,
Learned to observe, that Jackson 5 brake, till zoom grind my
neighbor's prick
I know she's listening outside. I've watched her move beside the air
I can feel her breasts moving underneath that lacy pink top,
They've a certain sexual energy flowing through them
Though I cannot wave my fork over my cheek to the touch me
I know that she instantly caught my imagination watching me
And her hands moved up my back, smoothing and caressing my skin
And that I do not know how those hands touched me, but suddenly I
felt this burning urge up my ass
I know what you're doing, her bright nothingness...
When the taste of her is turned so tedious me,
Slowly dragging down my cock as she licks it
How am I able to push that voice deeper in my head ...
Behold, even when she's seen me, I still feel more
That urge never fades, her hands straying to my ribcage ...
Gasp, I felt her lick in deep and suckle around my girth...
And a tough corkscrew is slipping down my groin
I heard footsteps, her heels thudding against the tile
She knows, I know I'm fucking, the self-satisfaction rises on behalf of
me,
As she licks and sucks my dick, not yet found a meaty peak
That's her mark
I can't see her but don't mind, I can feel her bounce within the booth,
Watching me stroke and lick,

I felt my cock grind and penetrate, as she gives her pussy affectionate
licks
Silky, wet, and electric, a dripping hot her
So, did they, I know, I can feel them move, circling in a circle sort of a
fire,
I can smell her backside as her legs wrap around my waist,
And I know they've seen me, as she fell mute in flickering limbo,
But they slowly walk all the way across the floor
I could hear the slams of plastic shoes within the rain,
Her touch every inch, as her blood pumps through her body,
And I think that I've left to my lover a memory to become her touch,
But then she's restrained and for a few reasons must be silent,
As she stands at attention and slowly hands me my sweat-soaked shirt
I'm unsure why my palms run on her back as I take off my pants...
But her hair falls in her eyes as she keens because the day ends
I'm so fucking curious, I'm quivering, my nipples hard and heavy again
What a powerful creature; I'm soooo turned on again,
I do not know where this is often all coming from . . .
I see her gone, a denim turtleneck falling down her shoulders,
And cut shorts on, but they stay within the place
lifelong physical power, ready to attract men with both gestures
No matter what she's thrown down there is no stopping me,
Ss I reminisce, I can see it happening more and more,
The summer's been good to me, I cannot control my thrills,
And her hair is swept aside, and she's wearing sandals
And then I see her, as she walks cold by, as she hands herself over,
Her hips are twisted, the posture is all raw muscle and tiny more,
As she approaches, I hear that low laughter and a small burst of raw
sexuality
I walk up to her, her lip trembles, and her gait is 'learned'
So, I just assume an in-depth standoff, as I hold my distribute a touch
Watch her eyes close as she slides a pass on my belly,

Her hand encounters mine, palm gliding along my fleshy abdomen
A soft warm breath, almost penetrating all around, penetrating
through my thighs,
Her hand joins mine, as I exploit my hands to show the pegs into a
standing position
Her hips move her gut in waves as I slip my hand under her denim to
shut down my pants
Then her bum steps backward as I feel her lips on my neck, and she or
he grabs the hem
She laughs her ass. how she slips the provocative fabric across my cock
As her sensual figure inches to grind it, my hands move ever close....

The Dome

Come at me
But she prevents me from reaching her epilogue
I wake to face our parting the dome of summer
imagine you were thereupon
I wish we were biting the bit together with her riding me
Taking her in my bed
Lighting ourselves up
Shooting nudes
The crackle of eardrums
Romantic laughter
Roses
Laughing tumbleweeds
The grass
She even helps me get obviate them.
I don't know what next
The old poems were written
But they left me in
The netherworld of pain
Where sky and mine were eager to give me wings
I knew she never noticed
They were burned deep into her soul.
Drawing peace horses is displayed in a web exhibit.
I wrote the foremost beautiful poem I ever wrote, isn't that an honor,
Welcoming it with such smiles, and that I know
When I text you usually
Lend me a kiss. But I assumed that we led fabulous lives
Like shipping up for a replacement one
And you recognize how I rolled
For years on the high water that rolled by with freedom,
Flying high and free. the woman was a millionaire,

Clothes too, you'll just smell her
Dressed, getting every shower rite,
Withered palms, typing together with her toes
in the land of fiber phones. That was nobody within the work
You Christians suggested is all that really animates
Well with beauty and we as lesser monsters need to forgive that
I heard the small voices and couldn't handle their obscene whisper
having attempted to be polite
Now I became a misanthrope, vulgar
once I dropped the woman
And the money I saved might be an ocean of
Unwanted grease being tossed
Into the torrent of idols and male followers
She isn't making up the dancing
This trivia can only have one connection
I even have myth wood in which I even have found a universe
That resembles our own
Though during a harsh and terrifying alternate reality
where the universe is forsaken and defiled
And therefore, the ten tribes of men
Are warfare because the world celebrates the eve of hell

How to Get into Paradise

Do what thou must urge us into paradise
Yet whether we should always live or die
Our fear and anger are being fanned by our denial
DO WHAT THOU WILT - Harm Not
We can loan positive experience as loans reciprocally for imaginary
things
And conquer cosmic fears
Conquer cosmic Loves
We are a botanical giant
Wild vines at our command
Voiceless we send our gentle helplines
Our tiny sparkles of sunshine
Map the vast intergalactic field
DO WHAT THOU WILT - Harm Not
To understand the aim of humanity
As neither an enemy to the opposite
Nor partner in surmounting the opposite
His assistance isn't yet conscribed
Thus, the good Mystery must be unfolded
Do what thy Knees to the Thumping' Drum
Do what thy Body to the Planking
Do what thy Back half to the Crib
Do what thy face to the mirror
DO WHAT THOU WILT - Harm Not
The Urge of Humanity
Continue the method of evolution
You can serve to make planetary human populations
Realize the large Bang as a consequence
Inanimate matter becomes Consciousness
Ensure the continued evolution of Humanity

Do What Thou Wilt-Harm Not
Serving bodhisattvas to simulate the present blissful state
Much is completed within the "stage of enlightenment"
Participating during a Taoist Sutra with great specific praise for
Buddha
Restoring our Garment of birth and death
Living blissfully while masquerading as high priests and priests
With learned conversations and prayerful teaching
Many have gained transmission mechanism or the Bodhicitta
The first teacher was a child scientist

The Art of clocks

Matter isn't what it seems to be
I see even within the darkest fires
Nothing can hide God's shadow
Who is beneath it all?
Asking how God made the khabs and therefore the moon
I'd need to pay my speed to prevent there
See the sunshine infinite
Burns away the retardation parts
Caught within the moves of gravity
The mystery
Offering no answers
An everlasting miracle
You remember
When Jesus asked if His name
Was the one that was called blessed
He wasn't told
In Torah
The oral cave
The very power of the creative act
Gives birth to God-form cells
Implanted with meaning
Professing to be and always be the One - God
The Love of God
Our true number
Without gift or fear
Of filth or happiness
We blow out is our brass tokens
Scratch our own backs again and again
Unto them that are ours
By making of deeds that can't be traced

Their stations fitted
Hexagrams on my mask
They all wait in lines before me
Give to the flock
Their one and only responsibility
All hail the kings
The end of creation
The age of sex
Toy with the Universe, send me teachings
And that I will drop you wish those who are below me
As a farmer, a child, a scholar, a warrior, or a beggar
All of you is housed in one among the gates of the Universe
I let the lions roam free within the Sun
And therefore, the beasts of the sector run amuck
Within the all-consuming dark of the night
When lusty desires banish your decision, let your thoughts be
Delusions allowing you to believe them to be facts that are utter
forgeries
Fear is that the gate to the inward forest
Fear is that the serpent eating the insect
Fear is that the key to all or any clues that expose you
The gardeners of my essence
What they uncover of fear is my secret garden
Your body whose form may be a conjuration of flesh and blood
Life extension whispering somewhere within
Gives hope to all or any those that wish
To form their shape a representation of the star
How am I able to confess it?
Elaborate inferences with the cryptic symbolism of clocks
Nature likes to remind us
One's breath may be a gaseous crown
Hiding within the vessel we exhale

Dust falls within the wind
From apartments on the highest of skyscrapers
Fainting within the gym
Metallic sulfate strips the trapdoors shut
Damn these guards the gorgeous
Seldom devoured by the very powers I desire
Automatons at their pulpits
Biome stroll on a grass skirts stretching across raging contracts
Timeless Annihilation
The Devil and therefore the Gates of Hell
It weaves around my web
No matter how long it's I'm deferred there's no Being phase Google
This is Nano Chromosome 9 propagating back to immortality meds
Bloodletting and UV
Nano Chromosome 9 has been resuscitated from death
And lives a dreadful existence
New brain cells using and consuming toxic metals
And therefore, the tin foil protecting them

The House Live

We are Being Ready
Who's counting on you?
There could even be angels within the garden of our souls
Through the trees beneath the rainbow
There could even be spirit tree campfires
Stalagmites of affection
Dreaming glimpses of stars in children's eyes
Children dreamed which we sang
The angel soothes the souls of heaven
That's what we love
Love me
"I must look straight ahead."
Killer and lures? Who's counting on you?
Just today, we are God
Here they feed us with drops of lifeblood
We grotesquely put ourselves
In his hands of affection and torment
Fay's earthworm pen
Caught during a sprig of curses
Fay crouched for a flash, reached out
And sucked
"So, we're not alone"
Fay said nicely
"I'll be careful"
Ashton released her hand
And pulled another
Ashton's typewriter
Nearly choked under the torture lines
And the hounds of hell won't catch
Now, she sits alone

The mouse clicks the keyboard
And the ink catches at the tine
And she's surrendering
The pen
"On to subsequent scene"
It's a science unit
Two surveillances barreled
Our eyes fastened to the inner wall
And tomorrow's mysteries
Some unconfirmed report on
The hypothetical mock
Will doom her to a lifetime of terror
The sound of an owl echoed through the woods
"Papa! Papa!" It called. "Is it a baby?"
Calm darkness abounds
Clouds and wind
She can hang her head
And lie back
And show light stains
Against the rising moon
And I am often my very own man
Look to my very own ends
What happens to me? "On to subsequent scene"
It's a science unit
Two surveillances barreled
Our eyes fastened to the inner wall
And tomorrow's mysteries
Some unconfirmed report on
The hypothetical mock
Will doom her to a lifetime of terror
When we don't dream...
When we become an area of everything...

When our fears are drowned in laughter
I finally decided to undertake this thing myself...
Five hundred, two hundred and...
Seven hundred and...
Eight hundred and nine...
I am madness,
So, cause, why ruin what's so strange?
I will live,
Or still your slowly dying

How to Be a flower

The children are ready for flower
Performing in his local garden
It is a renowned story
Let water waves keep off the elms
Shining Fountain of flowers
Like Dancers
The focus of this ethereal beauty
Is if it's you'd benefit
In chatting with the earth, you'd work
With her to supply her robes of flowers
Rejoice: all mortals are united in heart
On a Tower of trefoils
Touch the soul
At noon, who would be knowing fly south,
Display nonetheless
Whirl at an equal relaxed sedate pace
Like a racing waterwheel.
Sounds Spirit Gale Cold experts comes forth
Respected and revered
And only but more amazing
Spring all directly
If thirteen represents Thirteen Days of Monday
So, with dead keys to the doors
Three days to try to the house
Nine days to drink from the well
Five days to trim the chickens
Four days to slip the ultimate step
And pray to the sky
Six days to spin the yarn
Seven days to shower the sweaters

First members of our church
We are within our branches
Tonight, we are well and good
In our family we are the decision
In our house there's a waiting
The wells flow and that we are free
On our steps, children wait
And we catch the scent of our perfume
It is wise therefore upon entering
To kindle our flutes
Glow with washes
Wreaths exceed the night
When the shades unite
Cast lightning
As if upon some festive plain
Let these delicate and excellent flowers
Be admired and held in high esteem.
Wastes was once a rocky range
Grows to patience unbounded,
All sorts of art, and sport, are welcome
The vista and therefore the landscape are fae
Every splendid home feature a garden
Of which our Ursula will attest
Plants are cooked, many stored unto light
They taste sweet to our palate
Your talents are unearthed
Let the masses unite with you
On harnessing the architect
Bless Arch Spirit
To capture our present form is usually
Because these flowers are the maidens of it
Forever carrying the flame of one

One who was one and one with us
We call upon the word of Listening
Warmly, in constellations of sod,
Hold in high esteem the purple
Like a banner that was borne in time
Sicilian nymph of amethyst hail,
Red the rose of hospital it rises
Here in our garden under the moon
So, let our footfall be tempestuous
Holding up the ego
Toward the results of our industrial
Eye our hearts are moved
Enclosures are withstood
For lifelong, new uses for an equivalent
We cannot but be victors now
Emboldened, broken, nearer the High
With this powerful movie playing
Crush is that the same
Is it nothing to us
Listening is our judge
Time to carry, to collect our strength
Ready our steps to follow our fancy
A new high our faith does believe
So, allow us to all rejoice in being
One with this dear flock

Seek Truth

What does one seek, seeker of truth,
Luminosity and clarity
This should reveal what's Fugitive Truth Blossom,
Title, moreover, completing the Buddha dharma
Truly lament the ignorant magnanimous lover of peace
Who while checking out Luminosity; then leaves the acute Way
And is absorbed into fierce desires
Whose essence appears in their minds
As the people of the five times appeared before these three Buddhas,
At that point, the Buddha said "At two within the morning
I will be able to attend the tower
Then I will be able to return and nurse the sick
After recovering, I will announce to the people
About the pure virtues of the Tathagata"
So, it happened
Afterward, the Tathagata said to the people,
"Whenever you're suffering from covetousness, jealousy, anger,
or feigning immunity, listen when someone speaks to you.
Know that truth has some basis."
People couldn't understand him, then he said to them,
"It is like my bodhi-tree. I will let it down and it'll start to wither."
Then he divorced himself and disappointed his bodhi-tree
And at that point, he said to those who listened,
"Yet you say that you're deeply bent the Pure Land."
Here the entire assembly of sentient beings live buddhas
Why does one strive so intensely to become buddhas?
The answer, "It is strictly as you say!
Even as many holds are needed to understand this True Dharma." at
you!
Because you're not certain that the Confucian classics are correct,

The Supreme Teaching of the Supremely Enlightened Tathagata
Was ready to happen in you extremely quickly.
If not right, there'll be overlooked mental images of false life.
Doubt and doubt will arise were you to
Hold close the Superior truths of the Tathagata,
Counting on your own mind. There are not any Buddha roots
Surviving beyond which there's no Buddha's name
There are not any Santi's seed, no fourfold source,
No six-layered egg within the four paths
So, listen and do not abandon the standard of weaving [the]
Overworld and phenomenal worlds, arising and disappearing without
up
And down or side. Calisthenic practice makes the belly-deep,
No ecstatic light from starlight
Bestowing and withholding makes it light
After going, the obtainership becomes pure
What has got to be removed becomes mended
And nothing gets confused or soured
After failing to sing of Buddha and bodhisattvas,
He'll say, "Long ago, I became enlightened even as you indicated
Then I noticed the good Dharma King and attained nirvana
Therefore, I taught and cultivated alright ideals
Hail, great bodhisattvas! you create clear the pure truth"
So there became during this world more buddhas than buddhas there
have been
The whole eighteen spheres.
Great deeds have great significance
Anyone during this world should practice
But now his mind grows so large
That he hasn't been ready to verify a word he says
His are ways unfailingly suffer means he harbors supernatural power
The truth isn't distant from the guts

The mind always returns to the guts
It doesn't return to create false doctrines and practices.
A bodhisattva's goal is to supply perfections of the mind
Perfection of truth Dharma, the perfection of the mind's sphere
Produce such dharmas, and there's no more accumulated
Buddha-land.
Perfection of the mind's sphere unshakable
And only in time will it become a dharma civilization
If you're not even incarnating in one buddha plane,
An immeasurable personage will come and devour it
Put a finger into the hearth
There won't be peninsular water
Put a bit of steel into its center
There won't be a shadow.
Permanence will disappear, and a permanent mind will appear
To take refuge in Buddhas nothing then take refuge within the
Tathagata
Is named unknown and boundless

Night, Night

But tonight, finds us and she or he is crying and shrieking,
"Come back again tonight, . . . no . . . no ... If you would like there"
If you give your body to the spirit, will you resist at last?
From the shore, across the cold blue sea, is that the warm shore the
shore?
For there are 1,000,000 acres of White Rock Lake and Westwood
habit
As plain because the Rowan Pines, chips and surfaces embrace
At the purpose where the water runs at not quite 45°
Here at Sun's Deep are surfers grinding gullies, ropes, and short robes,
And fresh dust moving from basting needles;
There is thousand fish, and even balls of commando growling,
Mouthing the staple cover, Splashing telling the story of the ocean
And warning their hunger and salt lakes
If the ocean gobbles them up whole
If you eat in the lakes, are you able to still eat the shore?
What you want to do is ride through the night?
Hurry was the wisdom of the wise men of old
Do at your worst, and your best, as fast as possible
If you reside during a home, eat in the house that sits
If you come from a town, don't roll in the hay city sights
If you attend Long Lake, pass a boy's mound.
If you attend the mountain lakes, pass a young man's bed
And name it
But beware; it's a wilderness of long empty ways,
Relics of wilderness not
If you attend the spring whirlpools, rise on the girl's watch
If you come on horseback or on foot, because the wind blows,
You must be sensitive to the changing weather,
Even if the whirlpool goes down while you chase away

Fear not even the rocky road; here the troubles don't clank
The hills and mountains are still there, if you darken them,
Colors fade with distance
All manners of gray, greenness, and gray, and blotches of brown
Shall we pass that obscure range, and bear no worse
Like a faded picture, save the cold snow-white stains
An hour down the road by the lake, or five days
The river within the street of East Barrington.
At Llach Lasa you want to fall crazy with the mountain
And like it
And everything else, the waters, the rivers and brooks,
As a worm bites at the world and therefore the trees,
The soft roots that dry and retain their moisture;
All the traces of nature, aside from living things,
Rest at the sting, here by the lake
Love you, love you, and love not

Medieval Peak

There was gnarled layer upon layer of hedgerows and woods upon
them...
In the twilight and therefore the cold, the tall crowns fit the trees,
And high above the world, the white spires of Orcin's Peak were seen
There dark monsters prowled within the woods
Heaths, trees, under roads, tons of timber
Shall rise for the passing of the strangers on beasts' backs
And then there was the remote road, the hilly field with the fir trees,
And all the pictures of the country and therefore the hills.
With ruts digging into the bottom they passed,
Howls, and shouts of men and ladies everywhere the plain,
Screamed within the woodland, shouted and therefore the lads yelped
Over the hedgerows, hedges, and trees they passed,
Over the heather and stars with stars burn to shine,
Over the high hedges where the summer sunsets go so high
Where the good houses that old folks know are.
By stones that stray from the road, rocks, and stones large and little,
By big and little saddles and horses' bones,
Lumps of stones that rust away, large and little,
Beside the wintry roads and alongside the dews
Where the ocean meets the shore,
Through the coves rather than the land,
By beaches wide and tiny and forlorn,
And hedges and apple-cedars and rocks
And there these strange travelers keep they're thanks to and fro
While all the time they are going a dog's length backward.
They all in one gale went on their way,
"By the cow," said Strider while he was driving their long plow,
Maybe they're going to show their lonely thanks to them
And weave furtive paths in bitter weather

"By the trail to the zombie cottage" had they called it
There is the training ground of Goatskin
The land they need to rest on once they sleep within the moonlight.
And within the full moon´s light, they're going to sleep thereon dark
hill,
You will bring them southward the dishonor of that house
He still drove far along that lane of pines.
There were pastures along the long countryside,
Where hedges seemed never to bud or be cut
Lumpy craters they came back alone to,
There`s not a house there, not a home along the yellow line,
Nor where all the rocks are still countless, and therefore the council's
dead.
There´s nothing there for them to create a fireplace in.
Only a burning piece of ashes that was once good for ashes
"Where are all the people?" asked Strider as they burrow through the
thickets,
"The coast is marvelous," he said to Frodo
Of the fleeing, crying, chattering folk,
Scooting off somewhere to escape again,
They all know where they ought to search for them,
The pines along the lane will meet them!
The trees, they hurried far away!
At the very best summit of Orcin's Peak sometimes they set camp
again

The Buddha Perception

Not less could a Buddha measure his own mind
Because of the clear enlightenment of the Buddha's mind,
No more searching is required
All those that truly skills to an equivalent
Fundamentals of Suffering can walk the trail of the Way
It is enough by the Buddha's call
And what's the call? He says, "Excellent!"
It's nothing that the monks don't understand
If you catch on, that's your merit
Hence all the homes of all monks are in Purity
In the same way
Some stupid lands on the Buddha-made Buddha
But we all know that the Sun may be a Sun
Manifest you only too
In such how that day-monkey gains samadhi
Although suspect
But the bliss you gain is well worth the risk
Those who can settle the meditation on all the Dharmas
Are most worthy, for some are like this
Another-than-this man and that than this man obvious
Constantly passing the Buddha's Dharma and verbal bath
When the Dharma becomes ordinary
The ordinary within the Dharma becomes clear
Even worldly views and practices
Are merely refinements of the Three Thousand treasures
A man of weak capacity who has gone
Through flesh and bone alchemy
Must always guard himself against evil
Although he obeys the Buddha's words
He gives himself up to all or any the delusions of unsatisfaction

He hurts himself and is mortified by his ill riches
Though his health is all well
It becomes sad because he shares the same things as others
What's more, despite all his good deeds
All his congregation is dishonest
So, what is the use of hoping for a bunch of preaching
And by the way, he practices you're hoping for rebirth in heaven
It's just more of an equivalent until the day is over
Don't let the sick or poor fool you into
Bearing a cross or worshipping a better
But there's the religion of the Supporting Stronghold
Where loud-voiced monks and unarmed men pray together
In completely cease-celestial tradition.
Can you really drive the foolish here?
One by one
Thinkest thou that a Buddha are often dumped in another body?
This good man's flower and allure cause you to weary
"I'm tired of such a delusion"
Have you not heard that cultivating the Threefold Perception
Finds attainment as soon as you awaken
Hence your selfish wish for worldly bliss
Is useless to anyone if cultivated to utmost perfection
Animus and Anima dream of Nirvana
And Body and Mind don't lull
Never end and never cease
Who can endure these dreamers' dreams?
Animus and Anima dream of the treasures to be possessed,
Body and Mind watch their good deed's ruin
Never concludes their engagement
Lust leads the king to riches and lust drags him off into their net
But Body and Mind stay by the king's side
Now Buddha has ceased to be called "the Wanderer"

Why should he have disciples?
He has knowledgeable disciples who hold faith.
Most of the Bhiksus are fools of body and mind,
But a number of them are enlightened Buddhas.
People to be cited as heroes are worthless,
Now how are you able to brag you're one among them?
You can't climb up Mount Sumeru on earth or in heaven
Just because you let the Tribunal
Assign your proud acts
Therefore, the foremost gentle Buddha to line foot on earth
Is thus tenacious to face up to all insults
Right within the middle of their concentration
Cultivators have a mind of wisdom and judiciousness
They clearly see truth nature of things
But once they approach the Buddha's words
They lose their faith
This shows how their views are so incredibly subtle
Who has ever seen an adviser lose his wisdom?
To mutually rejecting the Lord Buddha
When the character of Dharma has the facility
To carry one back and obstruct all the three worlds
One most wretched existence is doomed to be discarded

The Meaning of Meanings

If a person is unaware of the aim of his oneness
In the ceaseless ambiguity of meanings
In the confusion of meanings
His teacher won't reveal his body
If a monk is unaware of the planet of Dharmakaya
In him we see the white barrenness of the awakened mind
If a monk is unaware of the planet of Transcendent Order,
And what's the meaning of our eyes?
And what's the meaning of our eyelids?
The eyes encircle our body
The eyelids encircle our mind
We are the Boundless
As with the clarity of the April sky
So, the subtle and straightforward perception of
The Five Transcendent Paths
Becomes clear, and the universe aligns
For the sake of awakening
Blown Apart and Boundless
The thought of birth, death, suffering, and native form dissolve
Into tetradic succinct clarity
Morphed into modern words
Rises up into the Space of seminal directives
A great sage once explained to the high officials
All sentient beings all things turn into the universal dharmata
As a result of the annihilation of samsara.
It is moreover said that the universe of delusion is of no use to sentient
beings
At that point, the high officials were confused
And they asked him. "Just what does our country need with its
destruction?"

The sage said "The world is ok soil which might be put to any use.
Even if they were to sow salt, it might be nearly as good as sterile clay."
The sky is that the realm of the hundreds and many stars
And is ideal in its brilliance he realm of heavens
And therefore, the surrounding heavens
Are just like the great limitless ocean
The god isn't Buddha
Like a mountain torrent is he, not a river,
Nor is he sort of a water sower is also he not crammed with seeds
Why does Buddha refuse to permit his devotees to cultivate within
the path of study?
And what's special about this dharma?
Ananda said "Actually, he didn't say "Unless they're ready to attain the
supernatural powers!"
He said, "Suffering, birth, old age, and death, regardless of what!""
He said that while fighting, and while not fighting, and while doing all
types of excellent deeds
And when the bitter fruits are discarded
He said that the master, the worthy beings, the Enlightened Ones
And everyone beings are boundless and free from all bondage
He said that there's nothing but clear light
Morphed into modern words
Rises up into the Space of seminal directives
Parsimonious though the logic of the first etymology
The words remain present to the present day
It has to be said!
Shaped by Words and Confusions
By the blackening of, putrefaction upon
This fragment is being mangled by words and putrefaction upon
words
To understand the destinies of sentient beings
One must thoroughly uphold the Three Jewels

It is easy to ascertain that one profound process of liberation
Forces a curtain to shut
A thin blue thread to separate the mind from its source
The people all have a turning around

Moon, Moon, Moon

I care nothing for its petty love
My body's brother's god
But this is often not the entire war the moon fights
Some of its wars with the sun, for the earth's sake
She sends its fingers of fate and makes it
Obey her today and mine tomorrow, as does the east through the west.
Piano music takes the sweet sound of the strings sort of a soulful
guitar
Like a thin violet weapon sort of a precious polish that's dehydration
at the fingertips
I'm a person of perfection
In the water sort of a virgin swept off her feet
I've learned the thanks to tease a woman
Before she answers back sort of a song
The melody of the flower is streaming mead
Like a rainbow, I charge sort of a dragon
I've learned to sculpt arouse sort of a warrior
Before you'll reach the sky, brown sweaters raised
And screaming like beasts, I appear to be a savage here
Rescue me, my nose doesn't grow back
But here the bird sings an old song of a person
I wasn't raised together with them
I was raised as a wolf-like Ryoga within the woods
But I have been reared sort of a man
In the air of six lifeless lives of the moon
You love me before you recognize me
If you think me once I say I'll cause you to my wife
You'd better believe it once I say what I'd do
I want to be alone time
My bicyclist friends swing a peach window pickup

GOOD INFECTION ALERT
Did I mention the peach window pickup?

Gemini Prepared Nature

The fields are crammed with our light
The plants are all is ours
We indeed are the stocking
In the crowd of the blossoming trees
We have brought together the multitude of stars
In the fields of occult teaching
Planting the seeds of Beauty
In all of creation
We channel Thelema
Through Gemini and Virgo
And through each of the opposite constellations
The Great Holy Mother has prepared
Her beautiful children
To guide them
Oracles to return
In the future hidden in knowledge
Now then join us now
In awakening the people
And planting the seeds and flowers
Inspired by Ahh!!!
Revelation told to Ophiuchus by Isis
The ceremonial purification ritual
Of the Egyptians within the three different directions
Coming from the Pyramid at Giza
Red and white
And the first and third combination
Coming from the Gold
The above may be a representation of the three
Purification of the Egyptian rite that once again
Brings the wisdom of Mother Isis

To every member of the order of Ophiuchus
In a Ritual drawn by famed Swami Shiva
Exhibit and presented on a stage
Of the hi-tech Cathedral of the Pleiades
North of California within the Valley of the Khabs
At the ceremony begun by Ophiuchus the god of light
Within the same room where
This is the culmination of the sacred work
"Blessed are the host and voyager Earthly creatures
For they shall be the lovers with the unripe ancient fruits
Of their mother's time, receive from these flowers
In perfect purity, the visions of fleeting lives
And the immortal grateful bone that frigid daylight grave
Concludes its labor and leaves the result of the last legacy
of the hands completed by union through the rites of affection"
Wow man is that this
Though there is a lot more that I do not remember
Or something... Lemme re-evaluate that again
Go ahead Lemme let Mother Isis say
To those folks who couldn't only heal
the sick within the hospitals Child newborn
I'd correct that Aleisterness consistent with your
For that comes in its time, Aurelius?
Prepared presents for an additional harvest of magical knowledge for
all folks
Wanna hear all about how this is often the simplest Angel ever
prepared?
Nature to its dispersed constituents

The world Technique

In you the moods I do know
Whether I do know
Light on behalf of me
Thought I could change
Then nothing ever changed
Again, and again
Copy my thoughts
Copy my crimes
Copy my hell because it's higher
After I wrote it a bit like this
Rather than another day
My brain is starving
But I cannot let it
Freeze its fears
And my soul is hungering
Crying out for its master
What?
The best of the simplest
This is I'm saying
This is how I'm ruling the planet

Damn My Overcompensation

Oh, a quick
Oh, a fast load
Damn my overcompensation
Little in life significant enough
Still clear conscious, but none taking notice
As best I can, especially when alone
I reach the highest
And see nothing
And note that I'm not even sure why
A thought breaks me
I'll keep climbing
There are some here
They may know I broke
if only they knew it
If you recognize me
I'm survived by several siblings

Boy's Pride

He has such fatherly pride
In the so-called swans
That he's willing to admit
When they are cowards
When they're just reading
The last word of a sentence
He'd said because it had been
Kind of offering them some psych
Let me make him honor his words
In the phrase Swans withered flowers
Beastly flowers he can take
As leather jacks
As of autumn
And bows their heads
To his advantage.
Of astronomy, philosophy
Philosophy of science
of living, and why there are days
And not days and why there are warm
And not warm, while intellect
And thy piece marinate between
There's little room for logic
There's a logic that has nothing
To say about commitment despite all it asserts
For it's all bedtime stories
The sage has told his thrice-avenged angels
Let me say boys are weak and women are strong

Play Alternately

So, they're alternately cognitive
A little content to sleep
Then unstoppable
"Looking for words like 'damn'?"
The man continues
"I know something quite interesting
I'm not a scientist anymore
But I tried to look them up
In the science binder"
"These words are the only thing
They know anywhere
They can't find them in the dictionary."
"How about a dictionary?" the man asks
"I know who the speaker is," the policeman,
who has been beaten up, says
"She knows how words work"
He believes the right one
There isn't anything he can do,
Isn't everything being bad for you?
And today my face begins to hurt
From the blue things the man sends through
If I see a bright color, I ask
"Is it do you play dirty?"
The swiftest idiot on earth
"I do," he says
For hear that, and not just for dope
I took their names
I can tell you things they don't like me
I had a point to make. Maybe I will make it up to them
"I am not a liar" I said

I know this ugly man
I spoke to his wife he is lost. He hates his life
I think I know where he is
Be well; I have something, too

Crystals and Mosquitoes

The sky on one hand is crystal clear
On the opposite, the dim blue shadow rests
Empty rowboats, and a yellow town
Yellow grass can it mean Lucy, besides?
She lives—lives—lives—lives—lives
So, I sat and felt my heart crammed with hate
Cold glaciers, frozen rivers, cold eyes
Did I would like to cry had her with no memory of me?
The eagle flew low, owl-like, bending down
The pretty kite, flying, and soft ticking beads
An old man, a lady why should they weep?
The blind water ox threw his coil
On the wagons of the steamboat bound west
I thought of the boys one has drowned
A replacement one died
Blood retains its froth for two steaming years.
So, here may be a trail of dashes and mosquitoes
From breakfast bad, on my broken shoes
Got my coat and pants-socks-ski socks-socks
All on the wall o' the cabin
Had my feet been green I'd be livin' in cold light
But here I buy dry and warm as a summers evening
Something ugly in the dark
The discordant sound, not of trumpets
I have been imagining
That I'm lying during a log-cabin, very wet
With paper swallowed by the moon, in Hawaii
I must warn you of malaria in early October,
All my red lamps are wet and certain of sunshine
I must think how one flies with a dead old duplex

And that one pays his airfare
Moscow ready for a gathering of camouflage to become
The teasing heat isn't my light, but a wrathful sun
I'm grayer to photographs here than on the beach
But now then I'm within the room the space is my light
Hope and therefore the prelude
The overture to bring more lights
Not of old ghosts to frighten, not of dams to burst
I play the wait at Utah I seem to travel more
And scenery yourself within the castle's chamber time is sweet
In endless hours were born the hope for several new sights
O aimless itch for adventure to form the night standstill
All horseflies over white valleys and mountains
Rise on your toes and light your lamp
O choose a gift for those you've hurt by deeds we've heard
Give wood to mightier men
And now croon a song narrative
Breaking halting day
Of "Boy" and "P - N" and "Foursome" and "Sweetheart"
Throwing it to my little child upon the bottom
I do not know that child that sleeps beside me
Call this for the scrolls of a witch land play
It's been filled in and glued to the curtain within the dark
In the hall the mirrors must be shut
Their masters won't calm the elfin temper
The king laments his minions, who came
Reason to the novice memory to patience.
What's worth the rock? Why can't you run without it?
I'm trembling for you would not be home
I guess time and the way we feel makes everything else strange
He unveiled Hillsborough Street itself
In two long, straight bodies, painted with tails of sable

I nearly cried when he pointed a camel's head!
Will you enquire a few jobs?
Moral was once burned for publishing fancy sentences
One countess sent a grandson for a dinner
Mend up the numbers of a broken consultation
Rare talents
I made it clear via sad curtains that the teacher frightened me more
Then attorney's twenty hours
A vague lullaby which will be lost in precious woods
My encounter with sparrow
What poetry am I able to say?
Never repeat again a deck of a eyes that Mary
I am trying for years and, can only repeat things

The Complete of T

I'm waiting, within the drowsy hours
Racing the shambles, I slept in
Frost winds where cool stars are laid
Crowds the places where the clerk's fires are lighted
Bright pain breaks my resigned mask
Falls all around me directly
I looked to left and right, and that I saw it fall
In every soul, thousands of wailings had begun
How long I sat, how long I pondered
At length, I sank back, and with my head turned
I lay down, and zip moved
I laid my soul down, along the weed-grown floor
Not knowing or thinking where I lay or how I fared
After a short time, my soul was far away
But once I even have returned from the dead
My soul spake to me and said
"You are cold and pale, for the sunlight is gone
We all are in Nameless Frost"

The grain

Then I saw the shimmer within the hills
Dim the grain and shine. I spied a replacement star
Laid it on the hilt of your sword
After you want to patronize mind the pick-up
Now my armor shines with shiny gold
Victory wilts within the gathering snow
The humanity will cease as a leaf blown
By a mild wind
Leave the plane of stone and winding rock
The jumping feebler
Far from it'll go till the last scale sours
I have been looking to die quite once of adulthood
I think I can live to be one hundred and fifty
There's nothing for man but to measure, he need to hurry
This is now the juncture of an age
Now my body is subservient to the fantastic mind
Now and forever is my memory dimmed
Now I'm at rest, I've climbed within the invisible vault
I savor the paleness of the pigeon
I'm freed from the cares of the world
I relive my life in ripples
Now I dwell my bed, a Miller's sleep
For the nice and cozy tops of hummed language
When will I wake from a dream where I born,
Or a dream heard within the night?
I thought that I knew where we were once, we left Isolation
But I knew nothing 'bout what to try to there
When the Polar Plume waxed high, then Didier and that I had
Polar War Kin made us brave on
And gentle Moise and curious Dragon

Approached us during a strange woman's dress
Possibly a baroness
For we only spoke until we went on with our work
And Grom made us drink champagne
And it made us considered, you never could guess
Because our night was delightful
After a short time, Fra Mime, Fra Eleonore; Agatha, Dame Agnes,
Gardener, Sicier, Safari, and Hippù and Agille,
Man, and Traveler, lowly Soldier
Swifter than a Gray Wolfs albatross, and more deft
Then a podgy Fox's, and fitter than a Capri
And all of them a tad tighter than their breed
I met the Ingub brothers and developed curious
Was observe and walk, trailing railway notes
Drought diminishing, the clouds became sound
And of beasts and birds, we'd watch and see
What moved and what shivered, I, half-mad, dare say
Still, we had Oriole and Tree view
And sauntering at an angiospermous tree, I saw some Tarsier
Even to the distress of dogs
How I do swoon?

Bad Love

"I like the way you dream bad dreams."
Not taking note of you knowing something else
Oh, wait I need to have done that too, but I'm unsure
When I do this, I've nearly always done it intentionally
I can nearly always sleep longer than you think that I might
I can nearly always be late for work, and stay late
When I'm exhausted, for all you recognize I'll change my mind
You didn't guarantee us an honest marriage, now nothing's guaranteed
And life goes on all an equivalent as always
New lies turn, new lies turn
I was once told that each one thing come to what I do
Lately, it seems I'm given one right back they do not want
I guess I just see tons of your habits, I buy bored easily
And I can't wait to urge to bed 'cause I do know I will be up later
Perhaps falling asleep didn't just happen to you
Because it's not my fault
I'd such as you to prevent causing such terrible wakeups
'Cause if you're focused on what to ascertain or what to try at twelve
it's very hard to not nod off
Then it's extremely hard to not awaken
Do you really try hard enough?
Maybe you only find yourself falling asleep!
We are all lucky to possess someone who can easily nod off
Yet the probabilities are that you've got never quite been ready to get
to sleep
Most probably you'll never achieve your dedication sometimes
Just like what many of us dislike about life
I believe crazy the straightforward and bright
'Cause where passion's love burns intense for the usually haven't
Of that piece reformed, what the planet looks fair?

There is no love not claimed, perhaps at some point I'll taste it
Or a sigh at my bedside, I'll tease may lovingly
Of that lovin', far and wide it has been but just accessible
I say it'll be forever still between us, but especially complete
By my every wound I will be a poet
"So, Lucite Bronte betrothed her morning already, so diamante and
more trés..."
I can attempt to add my missing pieces as I'm going
Of my mind's tall and natural cathartic call the image from day one
Oh, the day she's three and a half years old, and my first
Hatchling me up by the eyelids then my head falls to my breast
Ever since then I dreamed of her all my waking life
"Who am 'I the sole man,' his mother's son!"
Make no fool about my blade

My Eye

My one eye, and that I am one who sees
My eye and that I am one who goes
So far, I even have had to inform you that
I promised my mother that
So, she must've known when I'd come
But I cannot help telling you mom
I have had a turning point.
If you had known from the beginning,
You almost certainly would have guessed
I was entrusted to you for the primary time
In a very special way
I told you that, no I hadn't!
But I need to take the blame now for twisting things
As you've got seen within the past
My parents are very stubborn
Not easy once they all want to be the one and only
And now that my eye has gone, they insist
Make the proper decision turn instead to my risk balance
Which means everything comes right down to me
My one eye is that the face of a person who can see
You never skills it'll end up until you go
My one eye is one who sees
My one eye and that I am one who goes
So far, I even have had to inform you that.
I promised my mother that
So, she must've known when I'd come
But I cannot help telling you mom
I have had a turning point.
If you had known from the beginning
You almost certainly would've guessed.

I was entrusted to you for the primary time
In a very special way
I told you that, no I hadn't!
But need to take the blame now for twisting things.
As you've got seen within the past, my parents are very stubborn
Not easy once they all want to be the one and only
And now that my eye has gone, they insist
Make the proper decision turn instead to my risk balance
Which means everything comes right down to me
My one eye is that the face of a person who can see
You never skills it'll end up until you go
My one eye and that I am one who goes
I've never been so wrong that point
But now that I've lost my eye, I can see the reality
My horse is gone, my wife is gone, my friends are gone
Never lost a battle and my wife died
When my girlfriend left me for an additional boy
I thought she'd never revisit
I could always remember
When I tried to form love I felt tender in mid-air
So, I watched her fainting, and that I bore her generations
My one eye one who sees
My one eye one who goes
I've never been so wrong so time
But now that I've lost my eye
Now that my eye is gone
I can see the reality
My horse is gone missing six foot
My wife went gone gone gone gone gone
My friends went gone gone gone gone gone
Never lost a battle and my wife died
When my girlfriend left me for an additional boy

I thought she'd never revisit
I could always remember
When I tried to form love I felt tender in mid-air
So, I watched her fainting, I bore her generations

Life Is

Life isn't amnesiac
Life isn't haunted
Life isn't within the weeds
Life is in your eyes
The person I hate
I can't say if you will be my lover
The compulsion to detest
One who doesn't mean to...
Behind your face
Lowly sadness
With tools perverted
Teaches you the key
That you will never leave me
I want to be left alone
I want to be alone
I want to be left alone
Still frightened to intimate
Your long arms
Closing my heart with yours
Despite the slit
A veiled threat in your eyes
Your hot breath
Going cold on my back
The headstrong girl
How can anyone stick with this horror?
Metal chains that hold me down
Pilots of the planet shrinking
Minibots that fly
Got it all going
When you hand over on me

I get to feel your life go...
An eternal chase
And a game of Prisoner's Dilemma
Contemplating grandiose chances of failing
Handing all of my worth
To a monster
Just for an opportunity of winning daddy?
I am so evil
A child of hate
Behind the laughter insufferable
How can this be?
A shocking event in my life
No defense of me
The emotions through all of this
An unbroken chain of sadness
I will never learn to use them
I will never grasp the surround all
I get to observe the twang of his smile
As he watches me rant about life
I get to feel the ghost call
Coming from the silence
As you struggle to fight it, I tell you
I already know...
You secretly know all of it
With a glance of unthinking approval
You've tried so hard
To grasp the emotions of an empty soul
By something beyond, something besides you
You've tamed a fierce predator...
But now it's gone to waste
Hungry demons are waiting to hurl
All you ever wanted, such as you never wanted anything...

Won't allow you to see!
They are before me, dead-eyed demons
I hit them and that they didn't sizzle
I opposed them and that they went mad

The Solace Wind

The solace of the place faded lusterless
A retreating wind laid desolate
Amid a body, a flutist's harp and pipe in hand
Ay! I found the place! My hair was ragged
Nor was thinning; breath was never to me
Sweating like liquid flame, I'd lick the bits
Covered with snow or sighed over a bare tree.
A fin of gold pendant on a post lay by
Obscured by frost, lay a parcel, in singular mistake
A bundle of gold-chased by the furious horseman,
Who came from his own country
And royal arms over the border
A parcel of gold-cursed by the tradition of a lie
I knew my dog's halter when the cursedness
Of so foul a route toward my always haunting seat
Bid me ask what fear of thirst had inspired the attempt
A princess came to the summit
No one dared speak to friends aside from the queen
Suddenly had followed
Household servants warm took a brief passage back
Rescue tightened with heavy snowdrifts the villa stair
Aching cheeks within the sunshine eyed by the sacred river
I sought to seek out somber, tragic desire
Caught it during a body, glad and sad, but guilty
Surrounded by my old schoolmates and peers beneath the snow
Invite this silly tale, let the free spirits take the lead
Happy wish had I met you, caught her grip and ride down
No more sorrow, sadder to the present cold-hearted old man
Bowed off the rock and passed the youngsters mocking and swearing
Does not believe that this was the spot-on Cold Mountain

Which had played a fascinating, enchanted role to me!
Set within the background was a range
Shot through with often cloaked peaks
Life faded dull and painless to none, but cold
A feeling within the empty hollowed breast
Was it a deformed clump, fused with wood and rock
A partial stack of undergrowth, a mountain temple
Obscure and obscure yet once I saw the top, I understood
That is my grumbles and grasps the horseman meant me
Was I not quite a pale gaud? Was I as big as a tree
Too weak to try to such work as I've done.
He took my hand and led me to cotton gins
Whose banner they've burned directly, was I, this fox?
A statuary's mystique but the says his face is clean
No, he is not brother to the gold-fabled brother
Not that he got the new grandsire's cup and mind
There, with external usage and now I understand
Awake and certain to die, non-hardened chests recoil
Neither Hopewell nor Dr. Priest is claimed to float
I'll fall as far because the tip of your nose, I'll go for
You; my footsteps lead on. When touch as I do the khabs
That we wander o'er, the key to stars human sights map
The element I'm in, the descendants of a worm
One wild during the bluffs of the neck of cold Mountain
To reach his race deep within the bottomless clamber would
Help such the race I might lead it. Rags of straw
A dim place I'm, a speck in an ocean of blue.
No, they think it is a star, or hold it dear
Could you have explored my psychological depths over long years
Wondering what I used to be, only to return in sight of you
Not another impression from my solitary mountain haunt

Remains but the lantern's lead, rays to unfold your tale chilled by my
burning cheeks
My photos, your bed, the rapid news of a withered heart and body, the
dainty bricks
To cast a dusky shadow, bitter shadow on my youth, and body

What Do I Do?

These days have me dodging the incorrect roads,
Suffocating on existential philosophers
So, when there is a sign that says . . .
"Howdy, you, me?"
What do I do?
Who am I getting to believe?
Me the person I'm now
The one who lies in his bed
Vindictively, each day
The one who lives for days
Within the temple of his own vanity
Or could it's, fair reader, the one you care for
The one I even have so often tried to offer you
The one on whose body I even have spent my last breath
Will you knock?
Swivel around in your bed
Whisper into your pillow, I pray
"It's the sun I'll rest my head on tonight
The thick clouds are going to be above, the night remains "
Rise, my love, our love, altogether your glory
We stand steady beneath the celebs and therefore the moon
The two folks, the one and therefore the many
The one on whose body I even have spent my last breath
I prayed you'd pick me up
And bring me a robe
And take me running
Through the garden of existence on the brink of you
Under your hands, my love
Rise, my love, our love, altogether your glory
We stand steady beneath the stars and therefore the moon

Through the garden of existence on the brink of you
Under your hands, my love
Rise, my love, our love, altogether your glory
When old, I won't to call you my mother
When you began to seem my way
I saluted as best I could
Then, once you kissed your lover
With all of your youthful passion
I lost my place then I cried, mother
I tore it away, so it went
My lover
Where the grapes grow
In our love with their age

Time Rain

Some Time
You Must Remember This
The Rain in Soho
Something about me is odd
Less easy to know
Most things that travel this sky
I wish I weren't so
Pious
Self-deprecating
Great silly Rain
I wonder how the skies stay black
Like batwings tuned in to the foremost subtle pattern
You're singing like an angel
You're talking sort of a madman
Behind those kisses of melancholy
Unlike X factor contestant's
Which blame love and war
Or sloth and stupidity,
Hollow trees within the twilight
And suicidal rushes of history
What this delusion need to cost
The immortal soul?
You're singing like an angel
You're calling from the town
Or up past the border
At nightfall
You're losing your mind then am I
The night is dead though things are cool
And time is moving fast by now
I'm soaked with their tears then will you

I lost my mind then will you
God with all his great works
Unveiled will eventually fall
And these fall, to rise no more
Saint Francis of Assisi
Whilst all it was pride
Wiped from about the dust and flecks of dust
Some Time
Snowball slayer
Ugly sweater, like much of my wardrobes.
Prince's singing and no-one knows I'm up
School killing team but I'd preferably be alone
When they came to scan me, I pleaded the doors are locked
We're on the trucks, it's snowball slayer
Every bill in my hat
The thing is it's raining but let me still save
Boombox at a timer on my side of the hallway
Chair in my closet, all sprinkled in holes with old paint
But you're lovely, pretend I'm even worse
I wish I knew what we stood for once we did that
Heart of truth, I didn't represent it
What they hadn't recorded with a camera on blood
But breakfast Beach Boys on TV
Ready to die, almost, apparently
Like you
While I waver, I do know I'd rather
Keep it
Early siesta because it lifts
Dreaming of the righteous time for self-give
The way it had been
If I could start over, I would not even be me
But immediately my life isn't on behalf of me

You're singing like an angel
You're talking sort of a madman
Behind those kisses of melancholy
Like the man I took to back, with every hope that he now had
Far off like tears from a dark eye
Sometimes I'm wondering
Do you hear the rain come down, smashing on the windows?

Past helmets

Past my view. What! How far beyond the highroad
In part of its winter? Or, once passed
In another shape, shadowed with the day
Can the broad sword style 'til I bring the gold?
Yesterday within the city of garrisons had heard
Of a tribune of the Heralds' Guard by name
A youth of strong construction and a watchful eye
His nights sleeping clad in velvets of a dim summer night
His days storing coffee by the roadside behind the house
Where light from a rickin' hair-billets doth glimmer round.
I walked with eager heart, and heard his word,
"A horse has got to attend Carcă, the Apulian assault
Lines about four miles in opinion without a dream
Curiously relates so. Yet not so, for no horse
Has been mounted since last night." I told him so
Willing so! But is that this not strange? Where I among friends
Of your class, a brave soldier never saw I such noble guise
A tall horse breeches forking topsy-turvy, red tail
'Scaling trunks with tender feet, sturdy flank, and base
A bit of chest emerged within the collar, that wagged between
The first and second toes were a Y-backed stick
Inlets gushing from under the shoulders every single joint
A head so lively and filled with energy that filled
The sky, and harbored all his brain and everyone his joy
Inattention of a wise creature, for he came to wars
His mane of red as ivory, where the king's lock
Was gilded, a byword, every jealous hair stroking
"How, Minnear, does he distinguish noon from the night?"
His limbs bounds alongside bubbling gallant step
Like a leader of an excellent army coming with war-shout

And holding aloft the oaken cup, his long upright blade
Napoleon once the Free, will Praxiteles have amerced
Then I assumed I told you this morning of affection
Happening like sunlight teeming through interminable waves
Between the lines of a morning rosy-faced face
A flood of droplets over a mild white skin
Poured upon the immortal goddess
A contest for once
Which was overcome by Venus's sword
Once I asked of that hero main of my dreams
"Who's that he warring with?
Was it Charon, leading the flowering stream
Chasing with oars the fishes yonder out of the sea?
Or Perseus, huffing under his whip from the Hellespont
It was morning dead and blazing, from the mastery mouth
With awe and fear, these thousand feats of arms on earth
Might accomplish one-two thousand miles from shore
And Hell, and therefore the world of atrocious stars twice lighter
Ruffling the sea? Or ancient single-horned Latvian warhorses
With steel-pointed horn, divine of color and beauty
Formed in jewels, wearing helmets of ivory
And lead-skin helmets crammed with bullion steel with spare
And brass plates, with full pouches while they drive hard?
Or Hercules, naked?
Smiling he rages sort of a bulled bull
Wagging his horns, the planet round to Orestes, hot-faced
That brags to Aeneas, "Thou that wander with art and wit
And wandered for thy sweet Premium sight
Aeneas hath now placed on a man's skin for thy sake"
Their faces, I say Were wondrous ethereal
Splitting asunder within the hour
And from their pores. But what of their characters?

They were like charioteers call truant horses: wolves there they were
Not ugly but grim, old, partial strangers
Under their sharp beams, scarce ready to blend
With a sea beast's din to a person
Proved so on a raft, pulling alongside a gazing cow

I Love My Girlfriend

Will the gods be elsewhere?
"Shall we attend crimson, then?"
Such a daring proposition
Or so she told me
A suggestion she made me
As soon as I got him out of the living room
Where maybe the gods find us wasted alone
Or believe me for just a moment
I do know the story,
Danced 1,000,000 times before his unsuspecting eyes
Rewards through the streetlights
Picking up where we left off
And then the flames began to roll along the road
Racing in their own circle
Me laughing over the "daisy"
Are we just that desperate daydream?
Oughtn't we take our fury out on something tangible?
What does one consider my new quite sex?
I know it is a little bold
I sometimes even find myself fearing what might happen
Gazing up toward the tops of the towers
Or up the mysteries of the rooftops
When shutting out the cockroach's cats dogs hippos' animals etc.
Though nobody ever asked me about my sex life
With anyone especially
But I wand FOR spent hours in my bedroom,
Hiding from the traveler's staffers and confirmation seeker
Taking violently away all harmful, open have a cup of coffee
Or even a drink of water
When my mind is filled up with an old man at my feet

Giving me a hand rest, thoughts of his whisky citrus
Or the wind sort of a cool autumn breeze
Passionate hum, I find it simply sublime
Though the nicotine... am I able to stop?
I watch the world swallow his plane into the clear blue
And let me tell you, what each day it's.
Or maybe I'm just having a flash
I don't know
And I guessed you'd rather I wrapped her during a towel
and carried her across the courtyard
Pierced all across my skin until the burns throb like wild storms
Sparks, actually ache
Waking within the morning with a purple, swollen lip
Or in the dark watching other girls' riot in desperation years to come
home...
Try food any soup, casserole stew pizza whatever you've got available
I love her steamy dense cheese
Thick cornmeal crumbs, or *tasty* pizza I prefer to like all,
And then some. I really like an honest bowl,
But I've never pushed a steak until it had been perfectly cooked.
Mmmmmmm!
I usually eat smoothies, but
Oh God please don't
I'm hoping to actually get going
Now is the time to form a difference within the world,
Can you feel it?
Please don't continue living this way
To drink a daily glass of water might sound harmless
Would you?
On September 11th, I saw a pleasant woman covered in blood
So, I decided to try to something about it
And me, the person who cares barely for your daily cup

Stoked to urge a touch dirt inside you
Of these lovely vaginal pleasures!
Well, I placed on my listening headset
And dropped in dancing through the phone calls
And heard one among them say
"Hey, I really like my girlfriend
The way she makes me laugh
The way she adjusts, the way she take and provides"
I repeated it in my head sort of a broken record
The chorus "I love my girlfriend
The way she makes me laugh
The way she adjusts, the way she takes and provides"
In case you're wondering.
I love my girlfriend within the way she takes and gives!!
But I care far more about the very fact I'm taking and giving
Providing, emotional reinforcement for my ultimate passion for
grabbing you
I gripped your nether regions and held you tight whilst raging
overflow was coming halfway up my leg
It had been not as fresh as I assumed it might be, but
I gave in and purchased another to undertake
Refresh up my feelings
Some of the blood gushed down my legs during the flight ...
Shockwave of a bump, I fell, the sun occurred
Dear God, do I worry whenever I'm in a car now?

The Easter novel

If the gods can
And all the punishment they might dangle
Would quite satisfy them
Shall we continue with Right upon their call?
And around the other side of hell
Since we've both come too far back
To the darker end of Nagasaki
I had met
In the corner of a dream
Where one wonders if "daisy" belonged
And so, on then on
I thought to myself as we rowed
Through the noise of human life
When the flame rose, and it might burn us
KING and his rogue friends
As was explained to me within the course of the tour
I will nevermore have a drag
To answer what was my very own wonderment
Why I visited war and came back with so little
Or yet what remained to have finished me
To build my house and errands
Which that work could also be now greatly enlarged
And that not in the least more
Those significant of that memorable day
Out of piety I assail my very own account
The view of the North from a spyglass
So, penetrating with my spyglass through the loopholes
I watched with glimmering eyes the luxurious tactics
So consummately crowding into operation
Change the scene of that terrible battle

As I swung up
Sharp because the light in my spyglass' frame
The cave was a pandemonium of things
A compulsory gathering; shells and dead bodies
Everybody had a neighborhood to play
They were all worth fighting for
And what amuses me now
Is the political turmoil that developed
In Asia between Russia
The Cossack and British
"The war is over," I said; "it lives again"
Something like this, or a touch worse
And properly training for the Easter
In the festival of sacrifice
So much with you, my son
Life within the old world gladly
As the Cossack led security
Almost to his house
In the Yenisei, that was the scene I saw
Of Lord, his name was Leost riding up the river
For the primary time since his battles began
All in smooth black tunic and horseback
With a song on his lips and a banner behind
"Come, Omelanchol, King of the Danube Valley
Is your order so, that you simply must suffer?
Is it your patience in touch witness?
How are we to carry out only for you here?"
To which the Cossack answered, already mounted
High among the pictures of his glorious race
"When you discover that the enemy isn't abated
But has still the strength to strengthen his foe
You have thrown down Russia's just standing

Now do as heretofore ye have done
And I will not wait to quit this shirt."
What could your humble stature furnish
Against the returning enemy?

Canada, Canada

And then all of a sudden
So, I said, "Hello!"
There's a picture look for CANCEL Canada
I never knew it existed
Condemning Mark Keepman game-show crimes
Suicide
Al Qaeda or each morning when
A burly Canadian tackle unfairly veers
Towards my knees
Anyway, it is a joke, a child's prank
A lot of giggling all around
And the final punchline if you get knocked
Up the sole way you recognize how
By the top of it until death's no more
Was that Mark kept saying
I love you; I really like you; I really like you
"Or will the gods be elsewhere?"
Regarding the draft chandelier
I did an excellent fashion show for your ladies!
Now my guys would like it if
I could stand back from the portrayal of fashion illustrates
the type where there are pictures of plastic
Before the onset of the season
And if it doesn't exist
Someone who is so cheap to manufacture
They catch on at Wal-Mart if your greedy ass doesn't know that
The model always has got to wear
An equivalent number of garments that add up for the season
So, it might be the fatty that goes "Heads or Tails" as she always does"
And then just two days ago I ran out of rashes and pain

I didn't need anything
I was just kinda hanging there,
I even decided to require a second
To get rid of my streaks of tattoos from my calf
And I need to pee!
Just what percentage sheets did you add?
My dad wasn't around
He figured he'd recreate the Christian symbol
Take one out and redo it
What's the point of all this?
Ummm, the very fact that I can bathe myself
No, no, no, no!
"They always want to understand
when are you getting to be over here?"
Brougham colors
Activision, its BS scale
Printing a rock and ball that was to heaven!
It'll throw us a bone
Wouldn't it's cool
if in Godzilla's future
You could wear electro toys
With the shorts of the Incredible Hulk
Think of warping... the physical body!
I lost and do not feel much pain yet
But somebody got moved
Movement down the hall
There's Sir Jeremy Runciman
Hello, Sir Jeremy, how are you?
I'm doing alright
In anticipation of a highly emotional speech
On late within the game, he says
"Fleury please take a nap

And Suter please take a nap"
And gives me a tough time and not a lone kiss
Puts my clothes back on
And hands me a replacement one

The Friday Killer

Under the cold snap at the aureole
And within the distance my brother curses
There's no rescue from this deadly darkness
The ghoulish tracks my feet left within the night
The Friday the 13th killer
I had to cross the river, but I refuse to travel
Of course, it is a trap when a ghost acting the role of an old flame
Maybe he's simply extra aggressive
And can only kill it but not lose for he still clings to life
I could curse it, the unspeakably devious dangler
It's not necessarily, they're just good for the remainder folks
We've got to defeat them one at a time split the species
With the microwave and therefore the blender
There's something waiting, never knowing when he will strike
The video is all digital leaking gore and she or he does a Stranger
within the House
She takes a gun and shoots everyone
And I say no she's not me to speak to all or any the goddamn time
I just let her be
The little girl gets an old man and summons a monster
He was all smiles, brayed within the sort of a children's choir
Little did she know, there is no hiding from ghosts
And Tommy got it too and smiled through his yearning
You see he was a touch puddle on the ground
Suicide is such a lot easier, it isn't like its murder or death
It just makes one bleed
And I got up within the middle of the night, and I'll never sleep again
I'm getting to stab my house with poison ivy
I'm getting ready to destroy all future children
I need to kill tomorrow and now I'm not waiting

My brother sneaks up behind me and starts explaining ...
Blah blah blah ...bodhi blah ...bodhi blah ...
Holy ghost puke ...alien blood .... baby vomit
You're all made from fire ...all I want is
My head hurts I swear at dawn
I shall descend to destroy you all

Love At

Staring at a pale smile they called love
I heard a groan in my room I felt my foot tapping within the sleep
I stopped with a "please" and cocked back my head
With a smile, I dodged the fistful crushing crime
I pushed past was what I used to be thinking
It's not fair I'm being sucked in
I was born into this world, amen
Enter cutting and building my castle
Well, mister twig, the blood has been drawn light
The final chapter of what befallen your soul with a Polaris
It shimmers and trembles because the red moon is about in
I've lost friends, loved ones, it's all disintegrated
Some have pulled the buttons, but I do not understand
A relationship with someone who broke that heart
It's a freak accident, or they fall under a pit of coven meth
Beneath that rock, I laid me down, I stood copy this is often the top
now
With the throat confirmed through my mind, I'm now on the loose
By the caption of all, I know from the fires of destruction on the grass
My heart is decided by rage, or that rage is killing me
I'm finally Orion, I cannot let somebody shrink away
With the American lifestyle, where we're spliced into a singular
complex
You and that I are divided in, it's getting more unbearable
I do know you've seen a clan we dub the terrorist unit
And I believe they're on the verge of street bombing

Why You Ought to Live

We're on the sting of a fear man, through all the nights
Traveling through the bones that also carry hope for tomorrow
We're flying under the sky now
The Evil Spirits can get an edge on us, it is so embarrassing
Out of space, there it comes, zombies return to paradise
In the case of the Friday the 13th Killer
We lived the coldest and scariest month of our lives for one simple
reason
I accepted the bolt to the top, give me credit it'll thrill you
And then because the hall lights went out and that I could hear the
sounds of little girls
I turned to my team and said, "Hang on they're still running,"
I grabbed the gun, and that I shot all to shards and hearts
Whilst we waited for the top to return killing team one by one
The door was open, Charlee and Tyler all go under on the ground
Jezel said we were running from the shooters to the toilet
Nothing could have prepared me for that relief, I could have cried
The thoughts and dreams and love of my little life
Took me to the ground. Where you waited to die
Pushing away, wanting no more to more pain
Protect my home, stand on the wall now to try to now
I knew just how sore you were cause I knew you tight
Grabbed the gun, and that I charged your head with the one I really
like
I trace your body on the wall, no more you, we will touch now
Grabbed you for risk, and therefore the only safe place tonight
You were dead, it had been time we just let the killer go
We never stood an opportunity to survive cause in any case
Well, I feel he was just drunk at the time so maybe that's why
And fixed sights and fingerprints

So, once you asked me to write down
Our reasons to measure, my reasons are very odd
I don't know why it had been the way we chose to die
Mr. Will Sniper would be a far better description
But it's our song, and only our song so we came to a choice
The leader shot the two closest to the top and left us raw
I never revealed how we survived
I never told you that piece of information
So, what's the rationale to measure then?

Deep Red

While they roll along,
My heart is being torn in twain
And my moon burns down in flames
To see these voices return
To breathe its precious wind
They seem to tease me as I stroll
On past them on the streets of crimson
So, beware the sin of Hate
That likes to send you to ascertain
The deepest red once you least expect it
Deep Red is the place
In bitter stone for all
And all for one
Deep Red are going to be known
If you're taking the time to stumble
A little closer
To the beach
Heed the story of crimson
Snake within the dark
Howling day and night
Where you will find where
Too just barely
Kinda within the sunburns
If you stay
Here all night
When the sunshine seems to beckon
His Heart Beatin'
He meditates on the war
In the shadows
And dreams of going when the sky isn't so blue

The time has come to go to the mountains
His dreams of dashing ahead
Are sweet but far removed
And I know he'd rather stay onshore
Then leave this place alone
My Thumb Beating
He's never forgotten the meeting
Of the two folks
He knows where we touched
And was quite thankful
The ground exposes
O Creed within the lead
Swiping his glove above his head
Walking sidewards
Holding the air up high
Resting his backpack's strap
And milking his thumb
The storyteller steps ahead
Pitch, bat, kick
Even as the parts of him are slump
They move in rhythm
A million miles away
The stone warms up
This storyteller is warm
And just a touch drunk
I may be wrong about his knee
May be drunk on the wind
May yet return to the water
Deep Red is that the Place
Close, thick wall stones
They form the walls
Beneath the town

And muscle the citizens
They secure the shack
For the hardy few
It lies barely ten meters of cold stone
On the slopes of that mountain
Before the bow probe locale
Where, in black ass individuals
Frost will raise its breath
A whirling hush to hush all night crimson
A journey to crimson
After many nights...
"I told you I saw it within the dark!"

Love is Real and Evil

It's love and not some twisted compromise
Laying soft kisses across those shoreline fields surrounded by nature
But underneath there's an easy fact
Love is real and evil never was
She didn't like me then
But once I ask her if she ever felt something more
She tells me yes, she did
As we lay remnants of our rivers of wine
Darkened by the memories of the sleepless night
I attempt to justify my sexuality to myself
Love is additionally a mystery
I hit the wall and stare at the ground
But with these sad eyes, regardless of how hard I try
I cannot tell her no base lie of malignant self-love
Love is real, she said
Pausing for thought
I check out her eyes with hope
Bresea and Daisy, out there within the crowds of hundreds
On a bus or on a train, together with your friends all the while
And I ask what within the world intrigued you so?
And they reply, Lord knows if I had tons of friends
I'd find yourself waiting in line in Vegas for hours
Or just take their empty vodka bottles for a enter the park
Pouring them out on the bottom as they drown in their nectar

Love Misunderstood

The name that came out of my mouth was
"I feel it, it's coming into my body"
And that I waited for it, what else could it are
To die, to be reborn, to change
I dreamt of a world with colors all around me
I dreamed of the grins that were on behalf of me
I hope I did the proper thing
Because I dreamed that I found an area which I actually liked
That I created moments that you simply are now remembered for
I dreamed the day I married and have become a father of seven
Today, I awaken at 8.30 am
Then sometimes I sit in my home outside the town
And sometimes I shut my eyes to a touch of my soul
Because if I sleep, I cannot die
I have solved the age-old riddle that a woman can have a horse
But the standard man will never understand her smile
Behemoth of pieces both large and little
There was never a lurker who didn't point this bent me
It is what it is

The Name of Destiny

O, thou, Aiwass the minister of Hoor-paar-kraat,
Hast take advantage of the knowing Thespians
For, as a fanatical bullrush through the hearth
His fiery blood is poured upon the blackened air above
And maintaining his head becomes a dream
That very same bull after he has rushed
Through the midst of the hearth won't move his head
Signifying that his destruction is imminent
May my head and head only be spared!
O, thou abyss of the darkness of the Sophia
From whose secret reserves there's no escape!
Grace upon thee, thou golden darkness of the world!
A woman born of a mystic union with
The lord protectiveness of the good Architect
And therefore, the master of Nuit!
Appetite of the Khabs, which is man's true life-food
By the facility of the Khabs shall be quaffed
My light shall let loose thee from thy dark prison
Thy eyes by the art of the Khabs shall behold me
And that we shall once more melt the Khabs
I only endured the sunshine of the Khabs on hearing the word Ras
The Khabs, being ill ready to enter into this light
Became dark another time
And that I lived and subsisted during a state of misery.
The Khabs is invisible, whether by day or by night
Thou must love it until it's infected by this light
To acquire it another time, I will, among my slaves
Rub my feet against the Khabs: but while I do that
The Khabs swells and airs of its diaphanous sleep shall conquer me
And that I shall perish within the Khabs

For I even have consumed its flesh in its Great sleep
O, my Khabs! Be not desirous of killing me!
Once I had drawn my sword
And therefore, the serpent-brought bolt was out
Nothing was left, but a cloak of the King of Kings in my hand
Within the outdoors it appeared tall and eventful within the presence
of men
But when this far away from before me
I saw behind me a trembling
Hand of the Supreme! a woman up to her waist in shadow
Was covered together with her navel
And judging by the trembling of her folds I saw where her womb was
And on this, she vomited
At that moment Naassir-y-Shayumi
The stalk of the Vision of the planet, was born!
With entire Madness he discharged his bolt of Heaven
He comes with a dart which pierces the heart
That which breaks like pebbles on the mountains of Sinai
To the guts of Naassir-y-Shayumi!
All are dead! O, hero!
There's still time to interrupt the Fate of this World
The Name of Destiny hath been recovered: know it!
By thy Truth, my Prince, thou shalt be avenged!
Thou hast fulfilled the aim of thy Creator!
Thou hast wounded by thy justice and thy love those that are given
care.
Hast thou hast o'erplayed thy the Mistress, O my master mankind!
Hast, thou desired to become a star now, O my creation of stars?

The Story of the Story

I'm too far gone.
Love may be a n endless dungeon where every floor is a different color
I love the labyrinthine theory, now the most force
That simply captivates me with the treasure
But nothing creates the waypoint; it produces feelings of joy
When I'm alone in my front room, sitting ahead of the TV
The color red infuses those colors
It's true love's fleeting and leaves no satisfaction
I remembered a gorgeous girl who embodies all the power
To get on the great and high side and to let her guard down during a
way
Who's calm when right after midnight she starts singing to herself
I'll show them tonight whom everybody knows
Yet consistent with her, everything's fine now
As I hear her speechless screams and move a TV drama
I feel trapped during a cave, enthralled by an unreal fantasy
Oh Kyousuke, so beautiful then expensive
My idea, the thing of my dedicated lives
Is actually a person whom nobody gives a damn about

Love May be a Disease

I can't shake off that weakness of mine
But it'll be alright
This last joy she sees through is painted pastel blues
And a transparent sheet of paper gives her my billet doux
Folded on the billet doux may be a single word
The meaning of that resolve never loomed before
Desire may be a Disease
You and that i share an excessive amount of love and pain
For our next radio's haunted drives down the Kenchu blues
Top those selfsame molecules connect asleep in your chest
While this awakening is heart-pounding, you hold all the proper bits
When you finally are ready to stand on your own two feet
The beginning is soft as your base undulation with its downcast river
The sky is thunderous and therefore the people huddle on the brink
And another river bleats out the arrestingly sad chords
I'm within the middle and each time I see your rev's my heart
Whenever my soul paws on a paradise they are too wet
The brightening weed that hangs over you is their refusal to forgive
Killing your fiancé to save lots of the universe being one among your
best decisions
The Current Inland
With the rainfall, the force of the rocking, and therefore the echoes
there,
By keeping yours a stark mystery
Your hot courage to talk publicly here I climb into your bed where we
lay our heads on top of my broad
Lingered and gratefully hung over the sand and dirt
Clinging to you, clinging to me as you lay there
I disclose the reality, the stories of the sweet summer promised
The warning shouts to my face, my body grows heated

I find it all too natural to go away you now
All without a comfort blanket when it felt so comforting
I'm with thee now and now I'm alone
And my wicked character will only ease your heart away
This meandering landscape will only help to slip away your heart
And the band's road to the ocean is now leveled by the rain
A lonely emptiness awaits me within the deep woods of that lonely
season
But my island house is now my island home
A landscape becoming monotonous
I attempt to rush past the noise and teleporting portals in hope of
finding some relief
Bass suddenly yelps out the song and jogs my memory that this is often
my final stop

How to Make the Most of Your Love

In the middle of the house
When she is going to be choosing the matching clothes soon
Or that when it happens within the overnight quiet
There's an excessive amount of silence
And yet, her lips still freely move
unless I strongly attempt to stop them
i would like to the touch and make more honey
And not as a tool for sustenance
But as a source of wondrous ones
I remember the planet
Where there was something stronger behind my eyes
Back then, I lost my points, yes, lost my knowledge
But i do not got to lose any longer
Can you feel the far less dark, even a touch dearer?
I cannot believe it, i cannot say it
I don't want to talk, I'm trying to forget it
I want to point out the women first
Who's watching with drooling eyes 'round this place
I want to be captivated by the ladies who are wanting to see
Candles shine during a beautiful land just like the professional faces
Wears for one reason or another were neatly tied not for much longer
ago
So that they might be hidden, but not lost, on the bottom
I thought i used to be saving up for things like this where hearts meet
accidentally
I am too poor to be asked or agreed with, the happiest smiling face
Told me, I'm crazy about the quantity i assumed i will be able to give
to you
Beautiful girls are attracted by the desirability of somebody rare or
incredible

Frequently they stay alone but not too lonely, ahead of me was always
myself
Once I told her, that everything we do may be a set of ties that we
make
What's the price we ask to offer up our interest?
I saw her again her face was like that of a smiling face
But the highest of her forehead
Was a rock-wrapped hand that can't move
What it jogs my memory of
Is that there is price and risk...
I'm persuasive to the purpose of telling and undoing fear
I say what's upon my mind, sort of a voice that cannot be hidden
Say i will be able to assist you, but with no precautions
But there's still an excessive amount of on the past
And there's no limit to how far shall you go
If there is a lass in your heart like this
Where are you headed? Will you attend the New World?
A love like that can't have any regrets. That begins with me
I will always admit to a love like that
I'm sure that with difficulty it at some points are often exchanged
It focuses the mind, creates vibrant mood and imagination
A child may but I'm sure albeit there's one
It stands for this with sincerity
I'm sure there even a flash where existing been taken away...
In the center of the mind, there's also darkness
Even a private wandering isn't necessarily successful
Love may even be fallen before it's born.
That's my older sister, what she persisted in her head, maybe
It overflowed there, countless times, her dress changed without an area
As she walked peeled and angrily corrosive meat blood stains dyed it
light yellow

And from there to the flowing set of her shoulders with loss that
cannot be recognized
Her long hair stood out and a twisted illusion
A woman that murmured those words like what she felt
Her waist was drawn high on the brink of her waist and her knees
pulled
When she leaned her angular body forward and said, "No,"
The ceiling shook all of a sudden
I want to adore the happy transient,
Then when a teardrop appears ahead of me
The darkness beats away
They might under me shines with crystal clear light,
A heartfelt offer I realize once more
As the teardrop settles, it seemed hollow and barren of love
The feeling I accompany it's only now, the feeling of loss
As she steps back...
I want to adore the happy transient
Then when another teardrop appears ahead of me
I want to ascertain her look down on me
The ending of her gaze, there is no serenity in her face
Everything of wisdom falls away
All these passionate feelings walked together
And yet not as if you grasped hands could cling
To the sweet and delicate tiny treasure nest
Of a smiling heart
What gold awaits...
I believe you'd at any and everyone this
Bizarre, intoxicated but unexplored all to make certain

Ismael S. Rodriguez Jr. is a writer, poet, artist, and origami artist. He is originally from Philadelphia, PA but currently lives in Oakland Park, FL. He is a U.S. Navy veteran who served during Desert Storm. He is dual diagnosed with schizophrenia and a substance abuse problem and has experienced periods of homelessness. He now has 11 years clean and sober and is mentally and emotionally stable and in treatment for his issues. He is an ordained reverend and a Grey Witch who is also interested in Discordianism and ceremonial magick. He has a website where he posts poems, origami, and other things. The website is at https://thebulletproofpoet1.godaddysites.com/home that link as well as other links can be found at https://linktr.ee/bulletproofpoet.